Jelly Boots Smelly Boots

BLOOMSBURY CHILDREN'S BOOKS
Bloomsbury Publishing Plc
50 Bedford Square, London, WC1B 3DP, UK

BLOOMSBURY, BLOOMSBURY CHILDREN'S BOOKS and the Diana logo
are trademarks of Bloomsbury Publishing Plc

First published in Great Britain in 2016 by Bloomsbury Publishing Plc
This paperback edition published in Great Britain in 2018 by Bloomsbury Publishing Plc

A catalogue record for this book is available from the British Library

ISBN: PB: 978-1-4088-7344-1; eBook: 978-1-4088-8559-8;

2 4 6 8 10 9 7 5 3 1

Printed and bound in China by Leo Paper Products, Heshan, Guangdong

MIX
Paper from
responsible sources
FSC® C020056

To find out more about our authors and books visit www.bloomsbury.com
and sign up for our newsletters

Jelly Boots Smelly Boots

Michael Rosen

ILLUSTRATED BY

David Tazzyman

BLOOMSBURY
CHILDREN'S BOOKS
LONDON OXFORD NEW YORK NEW DELHI SYDNEY

Contents

Welly Boots

Welly boots
smelly boots
fill them up with
jelly boots

Welly boots
smelly boots
see them on the
telly boots

Welly boots
smelly boots
now they're in my
belly boots.

Down behind the dustbin
I met a dog called Dave.
He played in goal for us
and made a fantastic save.

Chicken Pox

What's the point of chicken pox?
Why don't they collect the spots
and put them in a box?
Then take the box far out of town,
dig a hole and put it in the ground.
I don't just mean my spots.
I mean everyone's chicken pox spots.

We'd have to find people to collect the spots –
not just a few, we'd need lots and lots.
We'd have to choose special spot collectors,
we'd need some special spot inspectors.
The inspectors would decide if it was chicken pox or not,
the collectors would collect every chicken pox spot,
put them in bags, take them to a chicken pox dump,
then scoop the spots up into a great big lump,
stick the lump in a box and shut the lid tight,
drive the box away in the middle of the night,
dig a great big hole and bury the box,
and that'd be the end of chicken pox.

The Competitions

Everywhere you go they have competitions;
my favourite is the one I hear
when I shut my eyes when I'm lying on the beach.
Actually there are two competitions.
The first one is:
Which seagull is the best at sounding like a baby crying?
The second one is:
Which baby is the best at sounding like a seagull?

The seagull that's best at sounding like a baby
says, 'WAAAAA!'
'You've won,' I say.
The baby that's best at sounding like a seagull
says, 'WAAAAA!'
'You've won,' I say.

WAAAA

After a while
all the seagulls sound like babies
and all the babies sound like seagulls.
'You've all won,' I say.

'Hurrah!' everyone says
and we all eat sandwiches.

'Hang on,' says somebody,
'that one sounds like a cat.'

WAAA

Finger Food

We went to a party and they said
that there wasn't going to be a meal
it was just 'finger food'.

Finger food?
Finger food???

Did they really think
I was going to eat finger food?

Nothing in the whole wide world
would make me eat finger food.

'No thank YOU!' I said.
'But you like nibbles,' they said.
'But not fingers,' I said.
'Finger food is not fingers,' they said,
'you just eat it with your fingers,
so it's called "finger food".'

But they couldn't trick me like that.
Underneath the crisps and the pretzels
and the nuts and the raisins
I could see fingers.
Hundreds and hundreds of fingers wiggling about
whispering, 'Eat me, eat me, eat me.'

Warning

I went to the shirt shop
and asked for a T-shirt.
They said we don't do T-shirts
we only do Coffee-shirts.
OK, I said, I'll have a Coffee-shirt.
I took my Coffee-shirt home,
went into my bedroom and
put it on. I started coughing.
I couldn't stop coughing:
cough, cough, cough,
cough, cough, cough, cough
cough.
I'm not getting a Coffee-shirt
again.

Question Mark

Our teacher said,
'This is a question mark;
where are you going to put it?'

We all had good ideas:
'In the red drawer.'
'In my pocket.'
'In my yellow pencil case.'
'On top of the cupboard.'

Our teacher said,
'No, we put a question mark
at the end of a question.
So now I want you to think of
a question and put a question mark
at the end of it.'
I said, 'Can I go to the toilet?'
'Correct,' said our teacher.
'No,' I said, 'I really do want to go
to the toilet.'

A Word

I know a word that isn't in the dictionary.
It's a word that comes from my dad.
It's a word that came from his grandfather.
It's a word that ... that ... I don't really know what
it means.
It's a word my father says
and he says he doesn't really know what it means.

All he knows is when to say it.
What he knows is when his grandfather
used to say it;
his grandfather who came from far away,
from a place he called 'The Heim'.

The word is:
'shnobbra-gants'.

My father says that his grandfather said it
when there was a big pile of food on the table
and everyone crowded round saying how nice
it was and started to eat it.

'Shnobbra-gants.'

I can imagine that.
All the old relatives crowding round a table
talking and laughing and my father is
a small boy trying to get to the table too,
pushing past the old relatives,
and his grandfather says,
'Shnobbra-gants!'

So when we have a big pile of food
on the table
and everyone crowds round saying how
nice it is and starts to eat it,
my dad says,
'Shnobbra-gants!'

One day someone said to me that
'gants' means 'goose'
and 'shnobbra' means 'beak'.

And when he said that,
all the old relatives turned into geese
at the edge of a forest
next to a lake
and they're all
flapping their wings and honking round the table
and my father turns into a small boy
trying to get to the table,
pushing past the geese.

The Toddlers

Look!
The toddlers are running away
The toddlers are on the run
Look at them on the beaches
Look at them in the sun.

It's toddlers in supermarkets
toddlers in the mall
It's toddlers in the park
and toddlers with a ball.

Yes!
The toddlers are on the run
Toddlers running away
The toddlers are quick
Toddlers doing it today.

They've just learned how to talk
They've just learned how to walk
They've just learned feeding
now they've taken up speeding.

They think you'll never catch them
They think you're much too slow
They think you're much too tall
and you can't bend down low.

Hear them whoop, shout and scream
Hear them laugh, squeal and giggle
If you do manage to grab them
get set for toddlers to wriggle.

They've tasted the fun
They've tasted the sun
They're running away
They're doing it today
If it's in a park or in a shop
The toddlers just don't want it to stop.

A Cat

I'm a cat
and that's that.

I hear you say
I should be thinner.
I don't care
I want my dinner.
Can't you see
I think it's awful
when all you give me
is a tiny forkful?
Can't you see me being grateful
when you give me a massive plateful?

You see
I'm a cat
that wants to get fat
and that's that.

Down behind the dustbin
I met a dog called Grace.
I was on drums.
She was on bass.

I Don't Like

Mum, Mum
I don't like
crusty bums in my ted
I mean
best mums in my bread
I mean
stoat bombs in my crest
I mean
beast tums in my test
I mean
tomb crusts in my head
I mean, I mean,
What do I mean?
I mean
toast crumbs in my bed.
That's what I mean.

Trouble

Once my brother was in trouble
big, big trouble
and he was sent to his room
and I went upstairs to talk to him
and he told me how it was really,
really, really, really UNFAIR
and it was all Dad's fault
and didn't I agree it was all
Dad's fault?

And I felt sorry for my brother
and I wondered how I could help
and I thought, I know!
I could shout something really horrible
about our dad
and that would make my brother
feel better
because then my brother would know
that I was on his side.

So I thought,
What shall I shout?
I know!
I'll shout,
'STINKY OLD DAD!'
I'll shout it really, really loud
and that'll help,
that'll make my brother feel better.

So I stood up on my bed
and I started to shout,
'STINKY OLD DAD!'

But the thing is,
I only got as far as
'STINKY OLD DA–'
when Dad walked in.
Right in the middle of me
shouting that.
I stopped just in time.

The thing is,
Dad didn't hear me.
He just walked straight in
and had another go at my brother.
And all the time Dad was going on
and on and on and on and on
we were trying not to laugh.
We didn't dare look at each other,
but I could hear my brother
making tiny little snorty noises in his nose.
And I coughed to cover up my laughing.

Then Dad walked out.

And we fell into a great heap of giggles,
saying 'Stinky Old Da–! Stinky Old Da–!'
over and over again.

Arrows

Me and my friend Harrybo,
we were playing 'Arrows'.
You take the grass
that's got pointed tops.
You pull one off and
you throw it.
It can glide through the air
and if it lands on something soft
it can stick in …
In something like a jumper
or your hair.
We love playing 'Arrows'.

We found this open window
on the wall of the alley
by my house.

We stood back from the window
to see who could get an arrow
through the window.
First it was his turn
then mine.
Mostly they missed.
Then one went in.
'Yeahhh! Arrow!!!' we shouted.
Then we carried on.
Missing again and again.

All of a sudden
a man appeared in the alley.
It was the man we called Baldy.
He came marching up
and stood there in front of us.
He held out his hand.
He looked down at it.
'WHAT DO YOU THINK THIS IS, EH?'
he shouted.
We looked down.
There,
stuck between his fingers,
was ...
... an arrow!

He told us to clear off.
And we did.

Later,
when we sat down round at Harrybo's place,
we talked about how the arrow
must have gone whizzing through the window
and landed on his hand,
and we imagined him sitting there
and an arrow coming from nowhere
wheeeeeeeeeeeeeee
through the window
and just happening to land on his hand.
Wow!
What a shot!
And we laughed and laughed.

Then,
much later,
Harrybo said,
'I wonder whose arrow it was.
Yours or mine?'

And neither of us knew.
And neither of us will ever know.

Down behind the dustbin
I met a dog called Amy.
She wanted one of my books
but said she wouldn't pay me.

Flying Home

Flying home from holiday
Flying home from holiday
All of us together
All of us together

Landing at the airport
Landing at the airport
All of us together
All of us together

In the airport bus
In the airport bus
All of us together
All of us together

In the big hall
In the big hall
All of us together
All of us together

Then Mum goes one way
Dad goes the other way
Mum's got one passport
Dad's got another

We're with Mum
Dad's on his own
We go through.
So where's Dad now?

Waiting for Dad
Waiting for Dad
Mum's biting her lips
Waiting for Dad.

Waiting for Dad
Waiting for Dad
Mum holding our hands
Waiting for Dad.

Waiting for Dad
Waiting for Dad
Waiting for Dad
Then it's:

There he is!
There he is!
He's got through
He's got through

So it's:
All of us together
All of us together
Heading home
All of us together
Heading home.

Imagine

Imagine if your nails are nails
so every time they get long
you hammer them in a bit to make them short.

Imagine if your sink sinks
so every time you have a wash
it gets lower and lower.

Imagine if your painting does painting
so every time you look at it
you can see the painting painting itself.

Imagine if a letter is a letter
so every time a letter arrives in the morning
you open it up
and all there is in it is the letter 'a'
or the letter 'q'.

Imagine if the stars are stars
so every time you look up at the sky at night
all you can see are famous people from the movies.

The Frisbee

On a camping trip
my brother and me
invented the Frisbee.

Frisbees that spin as they fly,
as they zoom, as they dip.
A Frisbee: it's a disc, a satellite,
a UFO, a spaceship.

The Frisbee – it looks like it should hum
or whirr or buzz.
It doesn't even whisper. It flies and spins:
That's what it does.

On a camping trip
my brother and me
invented the Frisbee.

I was seven
my brother was eleven.

We were washing the dishes:
thin, lightweight picnic plates.
My brother and me got bored.
It was getting late.

So we started throwing plates,
plates that spin as they fly,
as they zoom, as they dip.
Look! That plate is a disc
a satellite, a spaceship.

A plate that looks like it should hum
or whirr or buzz.
It doesn't even whisper. It flies, it spins:
That's what it does.

No one knows
my brother and me
invented the Frisbee,
on a camping trip
in 1953.

Because we didn't ever tell anyone that's what we did.

The Map

I was holding the map
and the roads went right up
to the edge of the map
and met the lines on my hand.

I wonder if we could walk along
the roads on the map
and then walk along the lines
on my hand.

I could hold out my hand
and point to one of the lines
and say,
'This is the way to the park,
follow me!'

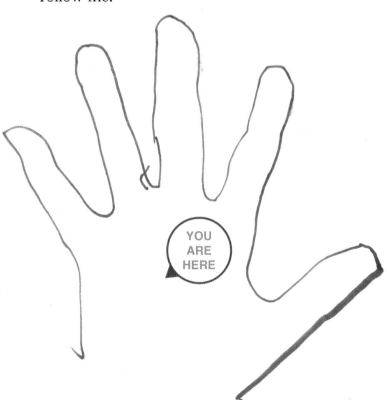

Orange

Help!
I'm stuck in an orange.
I can't get out.
It's really orange in here,
And wet.

Help!

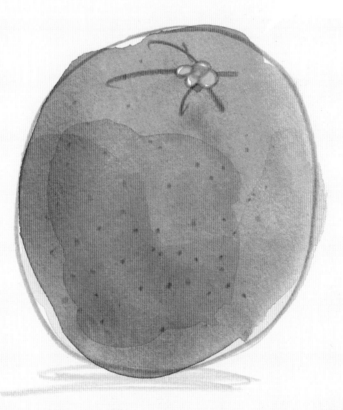

Breakfast

'I had samatter for breakfast.'
'What's "samatter"?'
'Nothing's the matter with me. What's the matter with you?'

'I had supp for breakfast.'
'What's "supp"?'
'Nothing's up with me. What's up with you?'

'I had spotheringyu for breakfast.'
'What's "spotheringyu"?'
'Nothing's bothering me. What's bothering you?'

'I had sappnin for breakfast.'
'What's "sappnin"?'
'Not a lot. Anything happening with you?'

I had sitallabout for breakfast.'
'What's "sitallabout"?'
'I don't know what it's all about. Do you?'

'I had sko-in-on for breakfast.'
'What's "sko-in-on"?'
'Not much. What's going on with you?'

'I had snotteezy for breakfast.'
'What's "snotteezy"?'
'It's not easy making up these jokes.'

In Bed

On Sundays
me and my brother stay in bed for ages
mucking about, telling stories
and Dad calls for us to come down
but we don't,
we go on mucking about, telling stories
and he comes rushing in and says,
'WHEN YOU WAKE UP,
GET UP!'

Now,
if one of us wakes up before the other one
we creep over to the other bed
where the other one is still fast asleep
put our mouth close to his ear
and shout,
'WHEN YOU WAKE UP,
GET UP!'

Down behind the dustbin
I met a dog called Mark.
'If I wasn't a dog,' he said,
'I'd like to be a shark.'

The People

My friend's dad took my friend and me
up a hill to see what he said was a
'People's Palace', a palace for the people.
We went for a ride on a little train round a lake
and we rowed to an island in the middle.
We looked out over the city and
my friend's dad said we had to believe in the people.
Down below us, an express train rushed along.
'That's the Tyne Tees Express,' he said,
'going all the way to Newcastle.'
It looked like it was as small as the little train we went on.
'Now I'll show you a secret,' he said.
Next to the People's Palace, there was a shed.
It was locked up. Railway lines led in.
We looked through a crack between the doors.
Inside there was an old train, shining in the dark.
A dark red railway engine with silver stripes.
'Maybe one day they'll get it out, and we
can ride round the lake being pulled by
that red and silver engine,' my friend's dad said.
'You have to have hope,' he said.

Q for a Poem

'Quack quack,' said the duck.
'Quick quick,' said the quail.
'Be quiet,' said the Queen.
'Don't quarrel,' said the snail.

'Aren't I first in the queue?'
said the Queen to the quail.
'What a silly question!'
said the duck to the snail.

'Quite right!' said the quads.
'Who asked you?' said the snail.
'Aren't I in charge?' said the
Queen.
'Is this a quiz?' said the quail.

Steam Train

We're on a steam train trip
We're on a steam train trip
Listen to the whistle blow
Pip! Pip! Pip!

Listen to our steam train
Go chuff chuff chuff
Listen to our steam train
Go puff puff puff

We wave out the window
We wave to the cars
And when it starts getting dark
We wave to the stars

Melon

Melon squashy
Melon sloshy
My friend Helen's
eating melon.
So far, so good
with Helen
and her melon.
But here's what I'm tellin'
Helen:
'Don't SIT on your melon,
Helen!'

Ships

A ship in a bottle
sails down the mantlepiece.
A ship in a photo
brings Granma here.
Ships they talk and talk about.
Ships far and near.

How did the ship
get in the bottle?
Ships by night and by day.
Ships they talk and talk about.
Why did Granma come to stay?

Who put the ship
in the bottle?

Ships that they once knew.
Ships they talk and talk about.
Why didn't Grandad come too?

When did the ship
go in the bottle?
Ships sailing far and near.
Ships they talk and talk about.
Who else didn't come here?

Who broke
the ship in the bottle?
Can anyone tell me why?
Ships they talk and talk about.
And why did the baby die?

Dad

Dad's a climbing frame.
We're climbing on Dad.
We've got a climbing frame.
Let's go mad.

The Checked Dress

I say, 'Will you wear the checked dress today?'
But Mum says, 'Not today.'

So I wait three days and then I say,
'Will you wear the checked dress today?'
She says, 'Yes', and I like it all day.

Before

Before I was born
I had two hands:

On one hand
one thumb.
On the other hand
another one.

In the middle of me
I had a heart.
It went
tcha-boom-sha
tcha-boom-sha
tcha-boom-sha.
My heart.

I had ears.
And my ears could hear
ca-boom
ca-boom
ca-boom.
My mum's heart.

Together we went
tcha-boom sha
tcha-boom sha
tcha-boom sha
ca-boom

tcha-boom sha
tcha-boom sha
tcha-boom sha
ca-boom ...

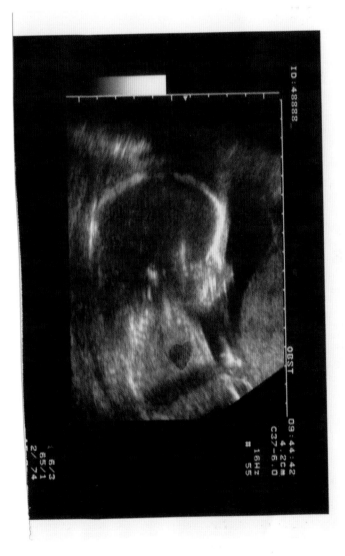

... before I was born.

The Cat

When we got a cat,
Dad said,
'Let's name him after a famous cat.'
He said that in one of his favourite books
there was a cat called Archy.

So we called our cat Archy.

I found my dad's favourite book.
It's called *Archy and Mehitabel*.
It's a really good book.
The thing is,
in the book, Archy is not a cat.
Mehitabel is the cat.
Archy is a cockroach.
Our black cat
is named after a famous cockroach.

He didn't mind.

A Dream

I sit down at a feast
the table is spread
with shining plates
silver knives and forks
candles burn
decorations glitter.

The food is waiting:
great big pies
bowls full of roast potatoes
pickles, chutneys, sauces,
jugfuls, dishfuls of hot food
cover the table
from end to end.

I reach forward
I'm ready to eat
but,
but,
what's this?
The pies are moving,
the bowls are moving,
the jugs and dishes
all moving
moving towards
me.

One of the pies
opens up, right in front of me,
there's a bowl,
sliding, sliding up to my hand.
A pie is going to eat me.
A bowl
has got hold of my finger.

DON'T DO IT!
DON'T DO IT!
LET GO!

A dish lands on my stomach:
PLOP!
and bites into me.
There's the jug
up at my face,

MIND MY EYES!

The pie is snapping round my neck.

GET OFF!!!!

I am not eating the dinner.
The dinner is eating me.
The
dinner
is
eating
me.
I wake up.

Bird song

Can you swallow a swallow?

Are you as swift as a swift?

Can you fly a kite with a kite?

Do you grouse about a grouse?

Have you ever stalked a stork?

Can you duck under a duck?

Are you ravin' about a raven?

Do you crow at a crow?

Does a puffin get you puffin'?

Do you howl at an owl?

Down behind the dustbin
I met a dog called Lizzy.
'Can you come here?' I said.
'No, I'm much too busy.'

My Brother

My brother's on the floor roaring.
My brother's on the floor roaring.
Why is my brother on the floor roaring?
My brother is on the floor roaring
because he's supposed to finish his beans
before he has his pudding.
But he doesn't want to finish his beans
before he has his pudding.
He says he wants his pudding
NOW!
But they won't let him.
So now,
my brother is on the floor roaring.

They're saying,
'I give you one more chance to finish those beans
or you don't go to Tony's.'
But he's not listening.
He's on the floor roaring.

He's getting told off.
I'm not.
I've eaten my beans.
And do you know what I'm doing now?
I'm eating my pudding.
And ...
he's on the floor roaring.

If he wasn't ...
... on the floor roaring,
he'd see me eating my pudding.
And if he looked really close
he might see a tiny little smile
at the corner of my mouth.
But he's not looking, because ...
... he's on the floor roaring.

Mum

Mum likes poems.
Mum likes bits of poems.
We might be sitting about doing nothing
and suddenly she looks up
and says in a sing-song voice,
'Tread softly because you tread on my dreams.'

We might be walking about
not doing anything special
and she suddenly waves her arm about
and says in her strange sing-song voice,
'Oh I am a cat that likes to
gallop about doing good!'
Mum likes poems.
Mum likes bits of poems.

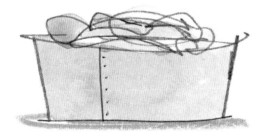

DinnerTime

Here is
the house where the rich man lives.
Here is
the fence the rich man put up
to stop his daughter going out.
Here is
the bridge his daughter crosses
with the poor man she loves
with the rich man chasing after them.
Here is
the boat they take to a far away place
where they are safe.
Here is
the house where they live together.
Here are
the trees that grow in their garden.
Here is
the house where the rich man lives
from where he sends out soldiers to find
his daughter and the poor man she loves.
Here are
the birds who were once the daughter
and the poor man she loves
flying across my plate.

Names

When we talk about
sisters and brothers
and fathers and mothers
when it comes to my dad
there's always a place
where there's a bit of a space.
It's a gap with no one there.
It's a father, a dad,
over there somewhere.

When we talk about
sisters and brothers
and fathers and mothers
and we get to the
sisters and brothers
of my father's father
he shuts his eyes
and says he'd rather
not talk about that.

But we ask for their names
and where they are
where do they live
and is it far?
And bit by bit
he tells us their names
none of them here
there was a war, he explains.

And we sit and we think
about us sitting here
how sisters and brothers
could just disappear
but because Mum and Dad
were in a different place
they could stay here
where they were safe
my mother and father
were able to survive
and here we are now
and we're all alive.

Judith

A friend of my dad's
comes from far, far away.
When she comes over
she'll often stay.

She comes upstairs
when I'm in bed
and asks me what was
the last book I read.

Then she looks out the window
and starts to talk
and when she talks
she starts to walk.

And as she walks
she scratches her nose
And as she scratches
she talks of volcanoes.

She says, 'We could hear
volcanoes talking ...'
Round and round my room
she's walking.

She says, 'We could hear
volcanoes moaning.'
She says, 'We could hear
volcanoes groaning

and one of the volcanoes
 – a very special one –
when this one talks
we have to run.'

She waves her hands
and then shouts, 'Boom!'
and now there's a volcano
in my room.

Yoyo

Mart's Mum was looking after me
but Mart wasn't there.
Mart's Mum said I could play with Mart's yoyo.
Mart's Mum said it was Mart's best yoyo.
Mart's Mum said, 'You can go outside and play with
Mart's best yoyo outside.'

I went outside with Mart's best yoyo.
I tried to do 'around the world'.
I tried to do 'walk the dog'.
Then I did my own thing with Mart's best yoyo.
I whirled it round and round above my head.
'I'm a helicopter,' I said.
I whirled Mart's best yoyo round and round
above my head.
Round and round and round.
Then I let go.
I didn't mean to let go of Mart's best yoyo.
Actually,
I don't think it was me who let go of Mart's best yoyo.
I think Mart's best yoyo let go of me.
Mart's best yoyo went flying through the air
over a fence
and then over another fence.
I don't know where Mart's best yoyo went.
It just went.

I went indoors.
Mart's Mum was looking at me.
I pretended I had Mart's best yoyo in my hand
and I stretched out my arm and pretended
to put Mart's best yoyo next to the biscuit jar.
Mart's Mum watched.
Mart's Mum went over to the biscuit jar.
'Where's the yoyo?' she said.
'It's gone,' I said.
'Gone?' she said.
'It just went,' I said.
'It just went? It just went? Where?' she said.
'I don't know,' I said.
'That was Mart's best yoyo,' Mart's Mum said.
'I know,' I said.

Eagle and Donkey

Donkey in the dingles,
eagle in the sky,
donkey does the cha-cha,
eagle can't fly.

Eagle and donkey
it's all gone wonky,
inky pinky ponky
plink plunk plonky.

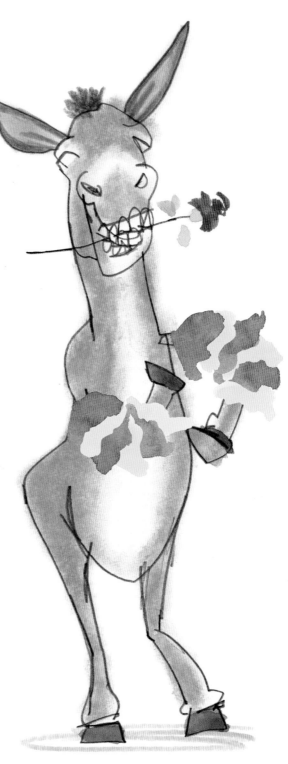

Panini

In my panini
something teeny.
Panini panini
something weeny.
Panini panini
bim bambini.

The Songs My Father Sings

When I shut my eyes
and go to sleep
I think of all sorts of things
I hear songs and bits of songs:
songs that my father sings.

How does he know all these songs?
Where has my father been?
Who sang the songs he sings
and what do the songs all mean?

'*Et hop Pipo, Pipo,*' from France

'*Simsalabim bambasala dusala dim,*' from Germany

'*Avanti o popolo,*' from Italy

'*Miss Mary Mack, Mack, Mack,*' from America

'*Linten adie, toorin adie,*' from Scotland

'*Mamita mia,*' from Spain

'*Kalinka, kalinka, kalinka moya,*' from Russia

'*With a hey and a ho and a hey nonny no,*' from England

and

'*Un di fidldik fidlers*

hobn fidldik gefidlt,

hobn fidldik gefidlt hobn zey,'

from his grandfather.

When I shut my eyes
and go to sleep
I think of all sorts of things
I hear songs and bits of songs:
songs that my father sings.

Lonely Lane

Don't ever go down to Lonely Lane
You know you won't ever come back again.
Lonely Lane is a lonely place
In Lonely Lane you have a lonely face

So come back home to Cheery Chops
Where everyone jumps and everyone hops
everyone leaps and everyone prances
everyone skips and everyone dances.

Metroland

I've seen the sign on the station wall
it's where we wait, it's where we stand
it's a sign that tells us where we live
a sign that says we're in 'Metroland'.

Metroland
Metroland

where the roads are long
and the trains go zing
the trams go clang
and the bus goes ping.

At night it's dark all along the roads
over the bridges the trains roll by
people inside can see me down here
the light of the train lights up the sky.

Metroland
Metroland

where the roads are long
and the trains go zing
the trams go clang
and the bus goes ping.

Like Robots

My brother took me to the Science Museum.
Upstairs in the Science Museum
there was a machine.
He explained that the machine
would show that when we speak, we sing.
My brother likes explaining things.

I put on some earphones.
A man in the earphones was talking like a robot,
never stopping, never changing his voice:
'... home Steve William's coming home Steve
William's coming home Steve William's coming ...'

'See?' my brother said. 'It doesn't make sense.
That shows that when we speak, we sing.
Singing helps us make sense.'
My brother likes explaining things.

On the way home, on the train,
we sat there doing the Science Museum thing,
talking like robots,
never stopping, never changing our voice:
'... home Steve William's coming home Steve
William's coming home Steve William's coming ...'

People looked at us. A man frowned.
They looked like they were wondering
what we were doing.

When we got home, we were having tea,
we sat there doing the Science Museum thing,
talking like robots,
never stopping, never changing our voice:
'... home Steve William's coming home Steve
William's coming home Steve William's coming ...'

'What are you two doing now?' Dad said.
'Not making sense,' my brother said.
My brother likes explaining things.

Mm?

Can you cancan on a can?
Can you cartwheel on a cart?
Will you whistle in the wind?
Have you heard it in your heart?

I can cancan on a can.
I can cartwheel on a cart.
I'll whistle in the wind.
I've heard it in my heart.

Could you keep what you could?
Would you wish that you would?
Did you do what you did?
Should you show what you should?

I could keep what I could.
I would wish what I would.
I did what I did.
I should show what I should.

Down behind the dustbin
I met a dog called James.
He says he's got two brothers

To

say this as quick as you can

to

two

too

tooth

toothpick

two toothpicks

two toothpicks too

it took two toothpicks to pick two teeth

it took two toothpicks to pick two teeth too

it took Tootie two toothpicks to pick two teeth too

it took Tootie in a tutu two toothpicks to pick two teeth too

Grandad's Complaining About His Cold

I really don't want to cause a kerfuffle
but I have to say I've got an awful snuffle
I'm walking along with a slow shuffle
I feel like my head is under a muffle
you could cheer me up with a chocolate truffle
but to tell the truth I've had more than enuffle.

The Dam on the Beach

A stream runs down the beach to the sea.
We paddle in the water, Martin and me.
Martin says we should build a dam.
He says, 'Are you ready?' I say, 'I am.'

And the sun is hot,
the water is cool,
if we build a dam,
we'll make a pool.

But we haven't got a spade to dig in the sand.
'No matter,' says Martin, 'just use your hand.'
The sand in the stream is soft and soggy.
We dig with our hands; it's gloopy and boggy.

And the sun is hot,
the water is cool,
if we build a dam,
we'll make a pool.

Handful by handful, we pile up the sand,
It's starting to look just as we planned.
Martin smooths it to look like concrete,
The heat on the beach is beginning to beat.

And the sun is hot,
the water is cool,
if we build a dam,
we'll make a pool.

The dam now stretches across the stream,
The heat in the air is making me dream.
Below the dam, it's starting to go dry,
I think the sun is eating the sky.

And the sun is hot,
the water is cool,
we've built a dam,
we're making a pool.

Above the dam, the water gets higher.
What if the sky turned into a fire?
The water in the pool could put it out.
Just then I hear Martin give a shout:

'We've built a dam,
we've made a pool.
The sun is hot
but the water's cool.'

'Come on,' he says, 'let's splash in the pool.
This is the way to get ourselves cool.'
We jumped in the water and danced about.
The fire in the sky started to go out.

But as we jumped, it washed away the sand.
This time it wasn't just as we planned:
the dam burst open, the water rushed through.
'You broke the dam!' said Mart. 'So did you!'

But we didn't mind, we stood in the flow,
the water in the pool dropped down low,
the stream went back to how it was before,
except for bits of the dam left on the shore.

We built a dam,
we made a pool.
The sun was hot
but the water was cool.

Metal Covers on the Pavement

On the pavement
there are metal covers,
like metal plates.
Sometimes there are metal messages
on the metal covers
saying who made them
and where,
like:
'Western Iron Works, Notting Hill.'
As we walk along, I start to wonder if there
are Eastern Iron Works too ...
or maybe Northern and Southern Iron Works as well.
And Notting Hill,
who goes notting up Notting Hill?
Does everyone say 'Not!' in Notting Hill?
'Are you alive?' you say.
'No, we're not,' they say. 'This is Notting Hill.'

Sometimes there are mysterious messages
on the metal plates,
like:
'Automatic Action'.
Does that mean that the metal plate
could leap in the air automatically
or could it spin round and round
automatically?

And sometimes there are mysterious words:
'hydrant',
'ductile',
'slideout',
'rapide'.

What do they mean?
I don't know.

And then there's one I see over and over.
It says:
'CATV'.

For a moment I thought it meant
that it was saying that it was
'Cat TV' and under the metal plate
there's a room where cats sit about
watching TV.
Maybe our cat goes out at night,
meets up with her friends, they lift the
metal plate
climb down and snuggle up to watch
Cat TV: whole programmes about cats,

trying to find which cat's got the talent,
Cat Olympics, Cat Football,
and Cat News.

But then I noticed it said CATV
not CAT TV
and I thought maybe it isn't CAT TV
after all.

Unless cats are not very good at spelling,
and they meant to write CAT TV
but wrote CATV by mistake.

Quiet

When people want me to be quiet
they shout 'Be quiet!' very loudly.

Down behind the dustbin
I met a dog called Peter.
'It's really cold today,
can you turn on the heater?'

Smells

I can tell
there's a smell.

There's perfume
in the room;

there's a scent
in the tent;

there's cologne
in the phone;

there's an odour
in the loader;

there's deodoriser
in the fertiliser.

I can tell
there's a smell.

The School Trip

We were going to go on a whole school trip.
The whole school was going to go on the river.
The whole school was going to go on a boat
and go down the river.

One teacher said that it would be a good idea
if we all learnt sea shanties.
I had never heard of sea shanties.
What's a sea shanty?

The teacher said it was a song that sailors used
to sing when they were hauling up the anchor,
or pulling on rope to make the sails go up on
a sailing ship.

I asked if we were going to be hauling up an
anchor or pulling on a rope to make the sails
go up on a sailing ship.

My teacher said that I must try much harder
not to be silly. The boat we're going on, she said,
doesn't have sails and someone else does the
anchor.

So every day in assembly we sang sea shanties.
We practised and practised and practised.
We sang, 'Oh Shenandoah, I love your daughter ...'

Who was Shenandoah and why did I love her
daughter? Or was it 'his' daughter?
I didn't get a chance to ask that question.

We loved singing it though:
'Oh Shenandoah, I love your daughter ...'

Then we sang, 'We're bound for the Rio Grande ...'
We all swayed to and fro when we sang that one.
'And away, boys, away,
A-way for Rio ...'

The Rio Grande sounded very grand.
So we were all very glad that we were going there.
I told my mum and dad and brother all about
Shenandoah and the Rio Grande.

After a few weeks, we all knew 'Shenandoah'
and 'Rio Grande' and we were ready to go on the
trip down the river.

It took us most of the day to get to the river
but the boat waited for us. We all got on board;
some people sat on top, some down below.

There was a man who told us what to see.
'There's the Tower of London,' he said.
'And there's Traitors' Gate.'

'Anyone who goes through Traitors' Gate,' he said,
'will never come out again.' He made it sound
as if we were all going to go through Traitors' Gate.

Maybe if I asked any more silly questions about sails and
anchors, I might have to go through
Traitors' Gate.

My friend asked me who was my favourite cowboy
on the television. I said that we didn't have a television
in my house, so he started telling me about all the
cowboys on his television:

Hank, the Cisco Kid, the Lone Ranger, Roy Rogers
and Hopalong Cassidy. He said his favourite was
Roy Rogers. I said that I liked the sound of
Hopalong Cassidy.

'Hopalong Cassidy,' I said.
'Hopalong, Hopalong,
Hopalong Cassidy.'
'Don't be silly,' he said.

Just then, the teachers started clapping their
hands together to get us to be quiet.
But it wasn't like at school, where everyone
could hear a teacher clapping.

Hardly anyone could hear them.
We were all talking about cowboys on the television.

Well, I don't suppose we all were, but some of us were, and other people were talking about other things like Muffin the Mule. Or Trebor Chews.

Trebor Chews were small sweets which when you put them in your mouth they made your teeth stick together.

Or Sharp's Strong Toffee. That made your teeth stick together too.

We had loads to talk about.

Anyway, the teachers wanted us to start singing the sea shanties. But we couldn't hear that they wanted us to start singing the sea shanties.

So they started to sing the sea shanties.
'Oh Shenandoah, I love your daughter ...'

Far away, I heard my teacher singing in her high voice, 'Oh Shenandoah, I love your daughter ...' and no one was joining in. Not even the good children who always join in. They were talking about Trebor Chews and Fizzy Refreshers.

So then the teachers gave up on 'Oh Shenandoah'
and started to sing 'Rio Grande':
'For we're bound for the Rio Grande
And away, boys, away,
A-way for Rio ...'

And they did lots of swaying. Big swaying.
They must have thought: that will get them going.
Everyone will sway and then everyone will sing.

But no one did. No one swayed. And no one sang
'We're bound for the Rio Grande'.

The boat went on.
We saw a crane.
Seagulls went 'Waaaaaaahhh!'
A train went over a bridge.
Then we spent the rest of the day going home.

When we got home, my mum and dad said,
'Did you have a good time?'
'Yes,' I said, 'a really good time.'

'What did you do?' my mum said.
'I talked about Roy Rogers,' I said, 'and
Hopalong Cassidy. Are we going to get a television?'

'No, not yet,' my mum said.
'Did you do anything else? Did you see anything good?'
'Yes,' I said, 'I saw Traitors' Gate.'

'You don't want to go in there, Mum,' I said,
'or you'll never come out.'
'No, I won't,' she said, 'don't you worry.'

'Did you sing the sea shanties?' she asked.
'No,' I said, 'we were talking about Trebor Chews.'
'Oh, that's a shame,' she said.
'I can sing it now,' I said.
'Oh, that's nice,' she said.

So me, Mum, Dad and my brother
sat and sang, 'Oh Shenandoah'
and 'We're bound for the Rio Grande'
and we ate egg on toast.

Down behind the dustbin
I met a dog called Dennis.
'I'm no good at football,
but I'm really good at tennis.'

Happy Song

Happy happy Gongday,
Bing bang bong
on your Gongday.
You'll never go wrong
on your Gongday.
You can sing your song
on your Gongday.
Sing it all day long
on your Gongday.
Sing it loud and strong
on your Gongday.
Happy happy Gongday.

Happy happy Songday
Bing bang bong
on your Songday.
You'll never go wrong
on your Songday.
You can sing your song
on your Songday.
Sing it all day long
on your Songday.
Sing it loud and strong
on your Songday.
Happy happy Songday.

My Cousins

My cousins are sisters.
When we go to their house
we do quizzes.

While my auntie cooks
my cousins
get out their quiz books.

'What do you call a baby parrot?'

'What colour is the common carrot?'

'What is the capital city of Spain?'

'Where in your body do you keep your brain?'

'What do you call a baby dog?'

'What do you call a baby frog?'

I start to get in a bit of a muddle,
my cousins sit together in a huddle,
they fire the questions faster and faster,
the quiz turns into a total disaster.

'What do you call a baby cow?'

'What do you think you're doing now?'

'What's the sea people call the "Med"?'

'Michael, why are you going red?'

'Who has a reindeer with the name of "Prancer"?'

'Michael, don't you know the answer?'

'What do you call a baby duck?'

'Why is it you think you're stuck?'

'Where's the moon?'

'Where's your spoon?'

'What's in the box?'

'When is a fox?'

'Why is a tree?'

'Where is tea?'

I say, 'I've had enough.'
I can't do any more of this stuff.
They say,
'In which country would you find the city of Rome?'
I say,
'I don't know. I want to go home.'

But then Auntie says it's time to eat,
she puts a cushion on my seat
we eat fresh warm bagels with sticky honey
my cousins do jokes I think are funny.
Auntie asks me why I'm wriggling,
my cousins say, 'Why are you giggling?'
They say to Auntie, 'Are our jokes better than his?'
And I say, 'Is that part of the quiz?'
Then we all do much more wriggling,
and then we all do much more giggling.

Joining Things Together

When the old, old people get together
sometimes they talk about when they were children.
Children?
How could they have been children?
In America, old, old cousin Ted, aged one hundred and one,
looks at a photo.
There's a family standing on a boat.
That's Granma.
Granma is standing with her children:
a baby, a little boy, a little girl.
The baby is Wallace, the girl is Sylvia,
the little boy is my father.
My father is a little boy?

The boat is sailing from America to England.
Old, old cousin Ted says he was there.
'How old were you?'
'fourteen,' he says, 'I was fourteen.'
He says,
'There was a trunk. An old black trunk.
I pulled that trunk on our cart
all the way to the railroad station.
Your Granma walked in front carrying the baby.
Sylvia walked with me, holding my left hand.
My right hand held the handle of the cart.
See your father? He's around three years old.
Sometimes he walked beside his mother,
your Granma,
sometimes he slowed down to walk with
his sister, Sylvia.
When we reached the railroad station,
there were about twenty steps to go up to the station.
I left the cart and the trunk at the bottom of the steps,
and helped your father and his sister up those steps.
The train had just pulled into the station.
I left the children at the top of the steps
and went down to get the trunk.
I had to pull the trunk on a rough road.
By the time I got back up to the station level,
the train was leaving.
I watched it leave.
Then I pulled the cart and the trunk
all the way back to our store.'
What's all this about the trunk?
Why are they talking about the trunk?

'Ah, the trunk,' my father says,
'full of photos of uncles and aunts and cousins
from America, France, Poland, Russia.'
'Where is it?' I say.
'Old, old cousin Ted says his father sent it on to England.'
'Where is it now?'
'Ah,' says my father, 'years later,
when Granma left the place she was living in,
she left it there by mistake.
When I went back, it had gone.'

'Did Granma go back to America?'
My father says, 'No, she never went back.'

Old, old cousin Ted says, 'No,
I never saw your Granma again.
She never came back.'

The railroad station, the cart, the trunk,
the boat, the flat.
Ted, Granma, my father, me.
I feel like I'm trying to join things together
that are far, far apart.

Then it's time for me to go.
'Bye, Ted,' I say. 'Thanks for everything,
thanks for telling me all those things, bye.'

My father says he doesn't remember
the railroad station. Or the boat.

Eat It or Leave It

If I push the peas round my plate
to see how fast they roll,
my dad says,
'Eat it or leave it.'
If I turn my mashed potato into a castle,
my dad says,
'Eat it or leave it.'
If I use the peas to turn the mashed potato
into a face,
my dad says,
'Eat it or leave it.'

When my dad spends ages and ages
and ages and ages
looking for fish bones in his fish,
I say,
'Eat it or leave it.'

Two Languages

Mum can speak two languages
and sometimes mixes them up.
She doesn't say, 'Don't moan!'
She says, 'Don't kvetch!'
She doesn't say, 'Don't slurp your soup!'
She says, 'Don't chup!'
(You say it so it nearly rhymes with soup.)
She doesn't say, 'Don't burp!'
She says, 'Don't graps!'
She doesn't say, 'Don't fart!'
She says, 'Don't fotz!'

When I have wrinkles in my socks
she says it looks like I've put my feet
through a pile of bagels,
so, she says:
'Take the bagels out of your socks!'

So I sing it all back to her:

Don't kvetch,
don't chup,
don't graps,
don't fotz.
Take the bagels
out of your socks.

We all sing it:

Don't kvetch
don't chup
don't graps
don't fotz.
Take the bagels
out of your socks.

Down behind the dustbin
I met a dog called Wayne.
He was throwing stuff
and generally being a pain.

Down behind the dustbin
I met that dog called Wayne.
I said, 'Oh-h-h no-o-o!
Not you again!'

Prune Stones

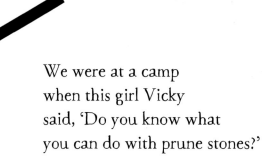

We were at a camp
when this girl Vicky
said, 'Do you know what
you can do with prune stones?'

She squeezed a prune stone
out of her mouth
and put it on the table.
She lifted up her spoon
and brought it down
as fast as she could
on to the prune stone.

It flew across the camp
at a million miles an hour.
It tore into a tent
and out the other side
flew through the flames
of the campfire
sizzling as it went
it shot through some trees
burning the leaves
headed for the nearby village
and when it got there
zoomed straight into
the church tower
hit the bell
and set it ringing like mad.

Old Joe Jump climbed up
the tower to try to get the bells
to stop ringing
but slipped on a prune stone
and came tumbling all
the way down.
Luckily he landed on
a donkey
who galloped off towards
our camp.
It galloped and galloped and galloped
and when it arrived
it went straight up to Vicky.
She was standing there
with the spoon in the air
just about to bring it down hard
on another prune stone.
But the donkey bent down
and ate it before she could
hit it.
Old Joe Jump said,
'What's for tea?'
and Vicky said, 'Prunes.'
'Hey,' said Old Joe Jump,
'I know something you can
do with prune stones.'

He squeezed a prune stone
out of his mouth
and put it on the table.
He lifted up his spoon
and brought it down
as fast as he could
on to the prune stone.

It flew across the camp
at a million miles an hour.
It tore into a tent
and out the other side
flew through the flames
of the campfire
sizzling as it went
it shot through some trees
burning the leaves
headed for the nearby village
and when it got there
zoomed straight into
the church tower
hit the bell
and set it ringing like mad.

Old Joe Jump climbed up
the tower to try to get the bells
to stop ringing
but slipped on a prune stone
and came tumbling all
the way down.
Luckily he landed on
a donkey
who galloped off towards
our camp.
It galloped and galloped and galloped
and when it arrived
it went straight up to Vicky.
She was standing there
with the spoon in the air
just about to bring it down hard
on another prune stone.
But the donkey bent down
and ate it before she could
hit it.
Old Joe Jump said,
'What's for tea?'
and Vicky said, 'Prunes.'
'Hey,' said Vicky,
'I know something you can
do with prune stones.'

She squeezed a prune stone
out of her mouth
and put it on the table.
She lifted up her spoon
and brought it down
as fast as she could
on to the prune stone.

It flew across the camp
at a million miles an hour ...

... you probably know what
happened next.

My Running Shoes

My running shoes are on the run
they've escaped from the room they were in
My running shoes are on the run
they're heading for the bin.

My running shoes are no good
I know that that's what they think
My running shoes are no good
they know they're starting to stink.

My running shoes are ashamed
They've decided it's best to go
My running shoes are ashamed
but they think that I don't know.

But oh I know all about them
I know that they're ashamed
I know all about them, oh yes,
it was something my socks explained.

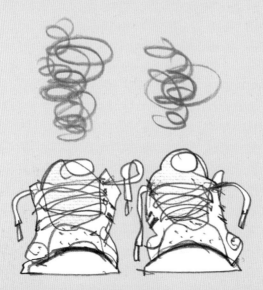

Our Cats

Our cats lick each other's faces.
Mum says they do that
because they're brothers.

I don't lick my brother's face
and he doesn't lick mine.

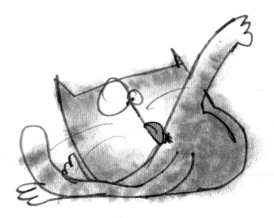

Plastic

My friend's dad
says that plastic is fantastic.
He says that you can make
anything out of plastic.
When I go round to his house
we eat our dinner off plastic plates
we chop up our food with plastic knives
and we eat with plastic forks
and plastic spoons
and we drink our drinks out of plastic cups.

He said that one day
in the future,
everything would be made of plastic.

My friend's mum said
it was time to eat now.
It was egg on toast.
I picked up my plastic knife
and plastic fork
and cut into my egg.
But the plastic fork
wouldn't stick into the egg
and the plastic knife
wouldn't cut the egg.

For a moment
I thought it was because
my plastic knife and fork
weren't good enough
to cut my egg.
Then I noticed that my friend's
mum and dad
were looking at me
and smiling.

I looked a bit more closely
at the egg.
It was a plastic egg.
My friend's mum and dad
said that it was a joke.
It was a joke egg.

I said to my friend's dad
maybe one day in the future
eggs would be made of plastic too.
That was a plastic joke.

*Down behind the dustbin
I met a dog called Neal.
I said, 'What you doing?'
He said, 'Keepin' it real.'*

Keep Moving

The loser's got lost
The freezer's got frost
The dancer's got to dance
on a ferry boat to France.

The chopper's got the chop
The shopper's got to shop
and the dancer's got to dance
on a ferry boat to France.

Good luck to the best
Good luck to the first
I might be the best
I might be the worst.

If I keep moving
I might get a chance,
and the dancer's got to dance
on a ferry boat to France.

ow!

Ow! That hurts,
you're pulling my hair!
Don't use that comb,
it hurts me just there …

… and there … and there.

Ow! I've only just got up,
it's still really early.
My hair hates that comb
because my hair's so curly …

… ow! … ow! … ow!

Ow! I've got a plan.
I'm going to shave my head.
All you'll be able to do
is polish my head instead …

… ha … ha … ha!

In the Lift

The voice in the lift says,
'This is the second floor,
stand clear of the door.'

Poor woman!
Stuck in the lift all day
every day,
saying:
'This is the second floor,
stand clear of the door.'

But where is she?
I can't see her.
I have a feeling
she's sitting on top of the lift
talking to us through the
ceiling.

But why can't she say
anything else today?
Like tell us some funny stories
or sing funny songs, like:

'I know an old bloke
and his name is Lord Jim.
He had a wife
who threw tomatoes at him.

Now, tomatoes are juicy,
don't injure the skin.
But these ones they did:
they were inside a tin.'

That would be a good one.
I wish she would sing it
while we're in the lift.

Friend

Ship

Words

Words are presents
that we give to each other.
You to your sister,
me to my brother,
your friends to you,
you to your friends,
on and on and on,
see, it never ends ...

The STOP Button

On the bus
there's a button that says,
STOP

What a strange button.
I wonder about it.

Is the STOP button saying to me,
'STOP WHAT YOU'RE DOING'?

If so,
how does it know
what I'm doing,
and how does it know
that I'm doing something
that I should stop?

I look closely at the
STOP button
and wonder how come
it knows so much?

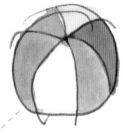

Down behind the dustbin
I met a dog called Andy.
He was sitting on the beach
and his bum was all sandy.